Bearded Dragons

BY ELIZABETH RAUM

Amicus High Interest is an imprint of Amicus
P.O. Box 1329, Mankato, MN 56002
www.amicuspublishing.us

Library of Congress Cataloging-in-Publication Data
Raum, Elizabeth.
 Bearded dragons / by Elizabeth Raum.
    pages cm.—(Lizards)
 Includes bibliographical references and index.
 Audience: Grades K to grade 3.
 Summary: "Describes bearded dragons, including what
they look like, where they live, some of their behaviors, how
they reproduce, and how they fit in the world"—Provided by
publisher.
 ISBN 978-1-60753-483-9 (library binding)—ISBN 978-1-
60753-696-3 (ebook)
 1. Bearded dragons (Reptiles)—Juvenile literature. I. Title.
 QL666.L223R38 2015
 597.95'5—dc23
                                           2013028236

Editor   Wendy Dieker
Series Designer   Kathleen Petelinsek
Book Designer   Heather Dreisbach
Photo Researcher   Kurtis Kinneman

Photo Credits: All photos Superstock except Alamy, Cover, 6–7,
23; Getty 5; Photoshot/NHPA 19; Shutterstock 10, 15, 24–25

Printed in the United States of America at Corporate Graphics
in North Mankato, Minnesota.

10 9 8 7 6 5 4 3 2

Table of Contents

A Scary Beard

A bearded dragon crawls across the Australian desert. He looks up. A hawk flies high above. Snakes and bigger lizards live nearby. They eat bearded dragons. So do **dingoes**, Australia's wild dogs. For the moment, the bearded dragon is safe. Then he spots a larger lizard in his path. It looks hungry.

A bearded dragon keeps
watch for predators.

The bearded dragon takes a
stand. He **inflates** his throat
pouch. Spiky scales stand out
all over it. It looks like the little
lizard has a dark beard. Next,
he opens his mouth wide.
The mouth is brightly colored.
Will this scare his enemy? Yes!
The other lizard scurries into
the bushes.

**This beardie tries to
scare away an enemy.**

There are seven different kinds, or **species**, of bearded dragons. Most are 13 to 24 inches (33 to 61 cm) long. They have long, chunky tails. They weigh 10 to 18 ounces (238.5 to 510 g). Their heads are shaped like triangles.

 Why is this lizard called a bearded dragon?

Look closely at the spiky scales on this beardie's chin.

 Its throat pouch looks like a beard when it is puffed up.

A grasshopper will make a good meal.

 Q Do bearded dragons eat more plants or animals?

What's for Dinner?

Bearded dragons have round bodies. Their stomachs are large. This lets them eat lots of food. Beardies are not picky eaters. They eat whatever they can find. Bearded dragons are **omnivores**. This means that they eat both plants and animals.

 They eat mostly insects.

Bearded dragons, like most lizards, have good eyesight. They are especially good at seeing moving objects. This helps them catch insects and spiders to eat. A beardie sees a bug. It flicks out its wide, sticky tongue. It grabs the bug. The bug sticks. The beardie munches the bug. Yum!

Sharp eyes help beardies
catch bugs to eat.

At Home in Australia

Bearded dragons live in Australia. Many live in the desert. Others live in woodlands or **savannas**. Some live near the shore. Their color matches the soil where they live. Desert beardies are usually sandy colored. Beardies that live in wooded areas are darker. Beardies change color very quickly.

 Why do beardies change color?

A beardie's color tends to match the place it lives in.

 Dark colors take in more heat from the sun. To stay warm, they may become darker. They get lighter when they want to cool off.

A bearded dragon finds a sunny spot to bask in.

Bearded lizards must stay warm. They cannot survive in cold temperatures. Australia suits them well. Even so, they **bask** in the sun to keep warm. They climb onto rocks, branches, or shrubs. Sometimes they even rest in the middle of the roads. The road stays warm longer than the ground.

Bearded dragons inflate their pouches to scare away enemies. They also flatten their bodies. Then they lift their heads and upper bodies off the ground. This makes them look bigger. They do not groan or make any sounds. But sometimes beardies lift a front leg and wave it in a circle.

 Why do they wave?

Beardies wave to scare away enemies.

 It's a beardie's way of saying, "Leave me alone. I don't want to fight."

Baby Beardies

Adult males bob their heads up and down when they are courting a female. They inflate their beards, too. If the female is not interested, she may wave. If she is, she bobs her head up and down slowly. Beardies usually mate during Australia's spring and summer. This happens from September to March.

Males and females come together to mate.

21

Female beardies bask before laying eggs. Basking makes eggs grow faster. When the eggs are ready, beardies dig a burrow 6 to 8 inches (15 to 20 cm) below ground. Each female lays up to 24 eggs at a time. After she lays her eggs, she covers the burrow with sand. Then she leaves the area.

 Are the eggs hard like bird eggs?

**Females lay leathery
eggs in a burrow.**

 No, the eggs are soft. They stretch
as the baby lizards grow inside them.

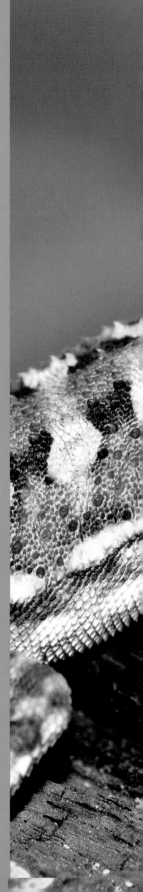

Beardie babies hatch 55 to 75 days later. They are very small, only 3 to 4 inches (7.5 to 10 cm) long. They must learn how to survive. Birds, snakes, or other lizards will try and eat them. They grow quickly and learn to defend themselves. If they survive, they will probably live 7 to 10 years.

Young beardies learn how to watch for enemies right away.

Bearded dragons can be good pets. But it is against the law to take them from the wild.

Well-Loved Beardies

Bearded dragons are not **endangered**. In the past, pet dealers caught bearded dragons. They took them out of Australia. Pet stores sold them as pets. Beardies were popular pets. They are gentle and friendly. And they are easy to care for. Today, laws stop pet dealers from taking bearded dragons out of Australia.

Even so, you may see bearded dragons in zoos or pet stores. These beardies never lived in Australia. Pet dealers **bred** them in the United States. You will have to go to Australia to see wild beardies. If you get too close, they may run and hide. They may inflate their beards and flatten their bodies. They may even wave.

Head to Australia to see a beardie like this in the wild.

Glossary

bask To lie in the sun to warm up.

bred To put a male and female together to produce babies.

dingo A wild dog that lives in Australia.

endangered Threatened or at risk of dying out.

inflate To puff out or swell up.

omnivore A person or animal that eats both plants and animals.

savanna An area of grassland with no trees.

species A kind or group of animals that share certain characteristics.

Read More

Buckingham, Suzanne. *Meet the Bearded Dragon.* New York: Rosen Publishing, 2009.

Rabe, Tish. *Miles and Miles of Reptiles.* New York: Random House, 2009.

Sirota, Lyn A. *Bearded Dragons.* Mankato, Minn.: Capstone Press, 2010.

Websites

Bearded Dragon
http://lllreptile.com/info/library/animal-care-sheets/ lizards-and-monitors/-/bearded-dragon/

Bearded Dragon—Oakland Zoo
http://www.oaklandzoo.org/Bearded_Dragon.php

Inland Bearded Dragon—National Zoological Park
http://nationalzoo.si.edu/Animals/ReptilesAmphibians /Facts/FactSheets/Inlandbeardeddragon.cfm

Index

About the Author

Elizabeth Raum has worked as a teacher, librarian, and writer. She has written dozens of books for young readers. She likes doing research and learning about new topics, and especially enjoyed learning about lizards. Even so, she doesn't want one for a pet! Dogs and cats are more cuddly. Visit her website at www.elizabethraum.net.